A SPRING IN ...

Poetry Collection By
Angel Wood

To April.
Best Wishes
Angel Wood

∞

Pyramid Images
Atlanta, GA

ISBN 978-0-9814660-0-2

PYRAMID IMAGES PUBLISHING, a division of Pyramid Images Inc.

First Pyramid Images Printing February 2008

Printed in the United States by Morris Publishing
3212 East Highway 30
Kearney, NE 68847
1-800-650-7888

For Jaire

ABOUT THE AUTHOR

Poet, playwright Angel Wood was born in Atlantic City, New Jersey. She moved into the projects of Dayton, Ohio with her family shortly thereafter. The Bella Vista Estates, where Angel called home, was a world of drug infestation and violence. It was a war zone and like any other war zone everybody leaves with scars. She had to deal with crack and heroine addiction in her own home, her family being torn apart, and her friends dying way too soon. Angel could have easily gone under with circumstance. Instead she chartered a new course, graduating high school with the highest grade point average in the city. She became the first person in her family to finish college, when she received her Bachelors Degree in Political Science and Criminal Justice from The Ohio State University. Angel started writing poetry very early in life as a way to express her thoughts and feelings. Poetry was a soul anchor for her as she navigated her way out of the projects. Even as gun shots rang outside of her bedroom window; Poetry offered an escape from the violence and confusion. In *A Spring in the Desert* Angel immortalizes those that she has loved and the ones she has lost - the many souls she has encountered along the way. Each piece, like a snapshot, captures a moment in time. It speaks to the pain that we all experience in this life and the hope that allows us to rise above even the most dismal circumstances. With the pen Angel found her voice and with her words she hopes to give voice to those who have yet to find theirs.

TABLE OF CONTENTS

The Love of Pen

A rainbow of colors course through you
Many unspeakable truths you have told
At times, you have bled black and then blue
An extension of soul be you that I hold
Connected are you to paths traveled in mind
Melody and poetry do drip from your fountain
Much neglected a voice in your scribe did find
Depth more than a valley
Greater strength than a mountain
Potent veins spill over uncontained to great release
You rise and fall to hit the mark
According to my contemplation
Electricity flows through my hand
When first you stain the leaf
I need you now to express to you my love in dedication
I wander if what for you I feel would be considered sin
You are but mere material, but my fate is to love a pen.

The Memory of Hope

Just the memory of hope
Is sufficient to revive a dying dream
It lives and breathes apart from reason
Hope's words to sanity's ear may ring as treason
Betraying all that is known of man
Existing within us but somehow apart
Integral to the survival of the heart, is hope.
It cannot die, truly
Of a rebellious sort, unruly
Never confined within the confines of precedent
Effervescent hope is not of the earth
But a gift lent from the heavens to us
Whose days would be in utter darkness without it
Do not doubt the resilience of hope
Although it is crushed it will again rise high within us
Like a cloud from the dust
Hope can live apart from joy
Exist alongside sorrow
Reach you at the point of death
And drag you into tomorrow
Hope can light the eye and dry the tear
And give life to a prayer
Hope whispers you are not alone
When no one else is there.

What I Have Known

I wondered often why it was that I was born
In my earliest memory my heart was torn
I have often questioned that spirit inside of me
That keeps getting me up and driving me forward
Towards greatness much bigger than me.

I had seen more than I should have seen- I thought
Endured more than I thought I could- But I fought

Still, I would not have grown how I have grown
Had I not known what I have known

I was the girl with no Daddy
So the predators in the hood thought they had me
Tomboy, rough and tumble push me I push back
Suffered the chaos and pain caused by another's affliction
That affliction was crack
Even though I never put the pipe to my lips to get high
Addiction found a way to make me cry

I had seen more than I should have seen- I thought
Endured more than I thought I could- But I fought

Still, I would not have grown how I have grown
Had I not known what I have known

I have loved that awesome love
And I have lost that awesome love

3

I held on to one so tight
That when he slipped away, I died
Then my heart did beat again
And I grieved my mourning's end
Walked the earth myself, alone
My soul mate here; my soul mate gone
I cursed the world unfair
Turned cold and tucked away my care
But compassion did return…and I went on

I had seen more than I should have seen- I thought
Endured more than I thought I could- But I fought

Still, I would not have grown how I have grown
Had I not known what I have known

I lost my song a time or two
And could not write to get me through
That may not mean a lot to you
But it is the Poet's pen that weeps
When the Poet cannot
The Poet's pen that keeps the Poet sane
Sometimes that Poet's pen- is all that Poet's got
Through the ink seeps out the pain
That otherwise might stay lodged and rot
The pressure mounted up so high
But not a tear fell from my eye
Was much too pissed to wonder why
My ink had fled, bled out and dried

I had seen more than I should have seen- I thought

Endured more than I thought I could- But I fought

Still, I would not have grown how I have grown
Had I not known what I have known.

Memory to Dust

My Memory was like a storm
Wild wind blowing
Untamed,
Weather worn
A flash of lightening
Once illuminating
Then striking
Setting all ablaze
Whatever blocked its path
Went up in a smoke haze
Thunder roaring
Threatening to drown all sound if not heard
Releasing the swells to flood through the streets
With one word
My Memory was like a storm
That caught me up and drenched me with its rain
Ignited a ring of fire around me
Commanded the sky to call my name
I fell in love with the storm
Its roar; the sweetest lullaby
I had no desire to be warmed
But the sun came up
And the sky went dry
Still, I will always remember
That once upon a time
I was showered by my Memory
While deep in the calm of the storm's eye
Then my storm ceased

No time to say goodbye
I know many long for sunny days
But not I
Heavens, bring back the rain
To quench this blazing pain
Its lightening was ferocious
And its hallowing winds rough
My memory was like a storm
But the sun with its searing heat
Evaporated the rain
And turned my Memory to dust.

A Tale of the Walk

Listen
I have a story to tell
About a babe that was learning
To walk when it fell
The Mother was in awe
Just a moment ago it seemed
That the babe had first begun to crawl
The Mother even found delight in the fall
But the babe could not understand
When it saw
Joy the Mother's eyes
All it felt was the pain
And it started to cry
The Mother lifted up her babe
And held it
Safely in her arms
The babe felt comforted
Cleared from the way of harm
But much to the babe's alarm
The Mother stood it
Yet again upon the floor
And challenged the babe
To try and walk once more
The babe was frightened
Remembering the pain
It seemed senseless to ever
Try and walk again
Maybe the babe could steady itself

Against the wall
Bend down slowly to the floor
The return to the crawl
So it would never again have to feel
The pain of the fall
And that the babe did
To the floor the babe slid
But the Mother stood it up
Once again tall
The babe realized then
No more an option was to crawl
It placed one foot
In front of the other
The babe started to make its way
Towards the arms of the Mother
The babe kept its eyes
On the hope
In the Mother's eyes
And its confidence grew
Due to the Mother's love for its try
No more was the babe's mind
Consumed with falling
Its ears were now fixed
On the sound of the Mother calling
Closer and closer to the Mother
Brought by each step the babe took
Its desire to reach its destination
Overcame the fear
But from newness its legs shook
The babe kept its eye
On the look in the Mother's eye

And it knew that if it fell
The Mother's hand would help it rise
Practicing day after day
The babe made its way
To the Mother's outreached hands
When finally it had mastered the walk
To the Mother's arms the babe ran.

The Day Before

I danced
Swept up by the rhythm of the drum
Smiling amid the setting sun
Twirling about
Just a swaying my hips
While libation slipped and dripped
From the tip of my lip
Jubilation and ecstasy
My warrior was watching me
Signaling loving and claiming
By stomping his feet
We both moved so quickly
To draw breath produced panting
The elders around us
Gave blessings through chanting
Could we bring them a son
By the next season's planting?
If I try very hard
I can hear my own laughter
I was married that day
Then the next, I was captured.

The Legacy

In the bowel of a ship
Set upon mid sea
I sighed A silent prayer for thee.
I may not make this journey alive,
But praise be to God that our faith survive.
As my skin is slit by the tip of the whip
Let the legacy of royalty erosion withstand.
Father, see us on to the Promised Land.
The lineage of greatness from which we hail
Will not be drowned along the miles we sail.
Destination unknown but our spiritual course is set.
No matter the method of persuasion
May the truth you not forget.
As Goliath, David slew
The Giant will fall at the sight of you.
Always keep in mind what you hold in your hands
And take every step like a conquering man.
Forget not the Legacy back to Abraham traced
Falter not from the rock upon which you are placed
Covenant withstanding whatever is to be faced
God chose us His people, we cannot be erased.
No force can crumble the foundation of God.
In silence I pass on to you my Staff and my Rod.

If Only I Could Fly

As I working in the field
One hot summer's day
A bird landed next to me
Then quickly flew away.
I fell down to my knees
And began to cry.

        Oh my Lord
        If only I could fly

If I could fly I would never land
In the sky I'd be safe
From whips of these wicked men.
I'd build my nest in the highest tree.
Up there no evilness could reach me.

I could use my wings
To fly back to the Mother Land.
Break free of these slave chains.
Be a man again.

Here in this strange land
There is no where to run.
Nowhere for me to hide.
I cannot swim away
God knows I've tried
But the ocean is too wide.

Here in this cruel land
I will surely die

    Oh my Lord
    If only I could fly

The Widow

The house stands bare
Set back from the road
She shivers and waits
On the porch in the cold
Emptiness clouds the air like dust
Will her love make it back from the war?
...He must
But lately the mailman fails to come
A letter a day has now dwindled to none
She imagined his countenance might turn weary
And worn
But she never imagined how his limbs
Would be torn
How his chest would cave
Or how soon would come the end of his days
A nervous knot lay in her stomach now
And her head aches much more
Than before the war
She thinks he has to make it back some how
So she keeps her post, in the chair, by the door
All those that used to come are gone
Still she sits, in the chair, by the door
Alone
Insane they say that still she waits
But he swore to her that he'd come back home.

Diary of a Slave Girl (Entry 1)

My eyes are weary
They have seen too much
My hands are bruised
And too sore to touch
My feet bare blisters
The road I have traveled is rough
My wooden cart they keep piling
Though it's full enough
The white scarf he gave me
Is soiled and red
I am to lay by the fire
The dirt floor is my bed
He has made me his whore
And not allowed me to wed
I can hear his steps coming
God strike him dead.

Diary of a Slave Girl (Entry 2)

Finally the rain has stopped
My eyes are void of a single tear drop
The fire once kindled
Is now smoke and ashes
Through the cracked door
I watch
As his carriage passes
All hope is dead
My wondering ceased
Quiet acceptance beginning
My numbness increased
The path that was given me
Lonely and dry
Belief in morality
Shattered
Though my head I hold high
The truth in my soul has accepted the lie
Soon I will gather the root
The master must die.

Diary of a Slave Girl (Entry 3)

Suddenly
It seemed
His health began failing
The doctor Misses sent for
Knew no cause for his ailing
They were holding out hope
That he soon would get well
Hope or not I had fixed him
Sent him early to hell
Just awhile before the master took ill
He told me
Cause he loved me
I could be free in his will
His skin once so pink
Quickly turned gray and ashen
I ground my liberation into dust
And sprinkled his rations.

Diary of a Slave Girl (Entry 4)

Under the cover of night
I wander
Towards the Promised Land
But a dream fills my satchel
Death stains my hands
And although it is wrong
To take away a life
I will not mourn that man
Most of my guilt I washed away
At the bank of the Chattahoochee
The rest is in a budding life
That grows and swells inside of me
I do not know what awaits us north
But I am certain that this one I bring forth
Since I made my escape
Its life has been saved
Dear God
My child won't be a slave.

My Past

I am searching
For a bridge
That connection
Suffering
In the absence
Of recollection
Sometimes
I get a glimpse
You
Calling to my soul
Through the rhythm
Of a drum
I hear you
I have waited for you
Yet, you have not come
I need
To know you thoroughly
Or else
I can not be truly
Me
I long to recover
All of me
Even the portion lost
Mid sea
Sometimes
I feel your pain
The explosion
Of sorrow and rage

Coming together
Like heated rain
Sometimes
The tears fall
So powerful
Is the desire
To possess you
At last
I want to recover
What has been stripped
From my being
I crave you
My past.

I Have a Heart

Do not turn on me now
Be you here for good
If only for awhile
It is hard enough for me to trust
I don't shine like I used to
Help me wipe away the dust
Do not turn on me now
Do not frown on me
Because I am found imperfect
Do not neglect or discard me
Just see, I am not the same me
You thought I'd be
When first you glimpsed my shell
Yes, I have been wounded
That happens when you walk through hell
Some scars remain
The wounds have healed
And I had strength enough
To not be killed
If it pains you too much
I won't speak of the pain
I will suffer in silence
Just let me remain
The speck of sorrow in my eye
Is laced with a trace of hope and faith
And though many tears have I cried
I am not empty
But full inside

Have empathy for me
But do not judge me
Keep your sympathy
Embrace me
Just face me
Do not erase me from your sight
I have fallen many times
Been scraped and bruised
But I'm alright
And fall again I might
But I will stand again upright
Remember me at night
When you take to your knees
And say whatever it is that you say
When you pray
Name me
Do not be ashamed of me
Do not turn away from
I am still here
Do not make void your senses
When I am calling
And you are near
Can't you hear?
Do not let fear cause you
To from me depart
I may not be all that I long to be
But still I have a heart.

Down Goes the Son

His eyes are hard
His pain is real
His soul is deep
He never sleeps

He lays awake at night
Wondering if he will live
To see tomorrow

His skin is brown
His heart is full of sorrow
He tries to think of a way out
As always he finds none

Up comes the son

The Lord has allowed him
To see another day
Run another play
In the game of life

Hours passed
Looking over his shoulder
Watching his back
Selling their crack

He craves to live
The so called normal life

Maybe have a dog, kids
Make his girl his wife

But that's a pipe dream
In the ghetto where he's from
So he doesn't think past twenty-one

Down goes the son

His eyes are still hard
His pain is still real
His soul remains deep

But in a hail of gun fire
It will all end
And tonight he will sleep.

The Night the Beat Stopped

One night the beat stopped
The baseline went still
I wondered if that piece of me
That was lulled to sleep
By the sudden silence
Would ever again wake
Or did my heart break
When the beat stopped

I was suspended
In the absence heard
Drowning in the dearth of word
Praying sound man bring the beat back
I had reached the end
Hoping that there would be
Just one more hidden track

But there was no more

If it were just scratched
Even if the scratch was deep
At least I could still hear the beat skip on repeat
Maybe it would have skipped hard
Jumped back to the beginning

But the CD was no longer spinning

They had shattered it
Broke it into so many pieces
There was nothing I could do

The night the beat stopped
I paused
Then in time
I went on
Finding that
Even though the beat is gone
I had memorized the song

Reality (Part 1)

Reality
Cuts deep
Like a knife
Sometimes it seems easier
To fantasize
Or rationalize
Then in comes life
Heartache
Strife
You tell yourself
You ain't sold your soul
It's not a problem
You can quit when you want to
You got this
It's under control
Then that witch
Addiction
Tightens her hold
You start to lose
What you forgot you had
Your looks go bad
There has to be another reason
For the decline
Cause in your mind
You got a handle on it all
Friends and family
Must be crazy
Gathering together

Conspiring
For your downfall
You ain't no junkie
Just a casual user
They need to try to rehab
Them real abusers
Like Sandy, Big Ray, and Lune
Stay hell out of your business
And let you handle you.

Reality (Part 2)

Reality
Cuts deep
Like a knife
Sometimes it seems easier
To fantasize
Or rationalize
Then in comes life
But you a soldier boy
You had to keep it real
Them niggas tried to clown you
Down you on your block
You had to grab that steel
Got a reputation to protect
You did what you had to do
Right?
Couldn't go out like no lame, Son
Daddy never taught you how to fist fight
But ooh, that fool pulled his strap
A little quicker than you
And he squeezed that trigger too
And there lay you
Don't worry about it
It's ok
At least you didn't go out like no sucka
Everybody in the hood
We got love for you Kid
But you still a dead mother...

False Notions of Me

Look at me
And for once see me
Free me completely
From the suffocating
False notions of me

Dare to peer
Beyond my flesh
Can you even fathom me?
A layered beauty
I am blessed

Accept as truth my spirit
Deny the rest
Do not pigeon-hole me
I will not fit
Recognize me with clarity
To mutual benefit

Take into account my whole
When figuring me
Calculate my soul
Please rescue me
From the bottomless hole
Dug with false notions of me

Ear to the Concrete

Got my ear to the concrete
Listening
Silent Hum
Of a dream come undone
Sun glistening
Burning hot
The haves and the have-nots separated
The latter regulated
By the ghetto bird
Search lights seen
Murder heard
From hide and go seek
Baby sister jumping rope
TO
Pistols blazing; cooking up dope
And eyes turned hard as steel
This game won't let you feel
Heart now bitter
COLD
Mama down on bended knee
Battling Satan for your soul
Prisoner of the train tracks to nowhere
Rage contained by gated streets
Shoeless feet
Stink of feces thickens the air
Found out before you could spell your name
Hell is real and life ain't fair
Want to make it out of the ghetto

But can't quite figure out how
Work from eight to five; go to school
Naw, you too used to fast money now
Daddy? Have no concept of him
Look just like him
But don't know him
To love him
No time for all that sentiment
You got dogs to walk
Outlined in chalk
Dying to be rich
Can't afford to think beyond the block
Got your hand on that fire
And a pocket full of rocks
CEMETERY
Steadily swelling
Concrete hum telling
TALE
Of a walk through living hell
Echoes of a lifeless form
Slain without a voice to yell.

I Demand to Know Why?

It is time that we had
A heart to heart talk
What exactly it is
About my style of walk
That makes me your target
An object of disrespect
I expect the enforcers of the law
To neglect to protect me
But not you
So now who?
I will not forget
How you violated my trust
My own, palmed me
Then stripped me
While caught up in a rush
On the news now whole panels
Convene to discuss us
Then you blame me
I'm at fault due to the way that I dress
But sisters in Africa were revered
Wearing much less than this
What lesson in history did you happen to miss?
How on Earth did my King get demoted to this?
When did the light of our love
Get overcome by the shade?
Whenever they see you they tremble
Now I too am afraid
I have stood beside you proudly

Since the Sun first began rising
When you hate me
Remember, it is you too you're despising
What a shame only I
Find your behavior surprising
When they labeled you evil
I screamed that a lie
Together before our heads were bowed
Picking cotton
Till we stared them dead in the eye
So when you turn on me Black Man
I DEMAND TO KNOW WHY?

No Place to Scream

Violence
Rocks the whole world over
Life of fear
Lived in fear
One eye ahead
One over your shoulder
Cannot truly say you lived
But your reflection
Appears much older
The tracks across your back
Make your eventual attack
Much colder
Not a piece of peace
To allow for much sleep
Heart breaks
When you awake
From a dream
Boxed in an out
Longing to shout
But you haven't a place
To scream

The Coldest Eye

The coldest eye
Ever beheld

Belonged to one whose heart had failed
Not yet grown but terminally battered
Powerless to blend his core was tattered

A man-child without grace
Oh, to look upon his face
One could mistake him for a child
But if any had chanced a second look
They would have seen his innocence was fouled

The coldest eye
Ever beheld

Suffered long in silence
And when the gun blast I yelled
Then my heart failed.

No One Came

You screamed once and no one came
Just a babe; you had no words for the pain
But knew to be ashamed
And ceased to scream again
Because once you did
And no one came

You looked not ever more
For a hand to sooth you
But plenty came when you grew
Tall and empty
Siphoning
While you were dying without empathy
Indifferent
Those hands could see but a shell
Temporarily cradling your body
As your Soul languished in hell
Smile relayed that all was well
Dimpled cheeks made joy easy to feign
But eyes betrayed
Portrayed a heart that went lame
Way back then, when no one came

Daily, silently praying to be laid down
That you might die
You shot death into your veins
Under the cover of getting high
The peace that found you

In that hazed release
Was an ever fleeting lie
Until finally you slipped away
Without a word

Goodbye.

For Tasha

Dissolution

Dissolution granted
Not a grain of resolution planted
Bitterness did slay the seed
But on flourished the need

DISSOLUTION

Fade to black
If one be of nothing
Then what should one lack
Everything if inborn be desire

DESIRE

Desire in absence is as fire
Laying waste to the forest
But much slower to retire
Is desire

DISSOLUTION

Is hallow
Vanquishing all preceding
Tainting that which follows

Not in total erased
A speck seen
In the carved lines of the face

But unrecognized
Evaporates to no place
Missing without a trace.

Knight's Canvas

A resigned soul
Drowned in a lake of fire
Eyes wide
Watching
Tears dried
Burning
Praying to retire
Guns blast like thread
Weaving holes
Through Knight's canvas
A promise conceived
That went fruitless
Painted red
Blood shed
Stained and splattered
An unfinished portrait
Of a dream shattered.

Into Your Eyes

If one gazed into your eyes
Too deep
They might discover the secrets
Which from the world you keep
Pain hidden far beyond the light
Screams of silence beginning
That stormy night
Innocence stolen
No reward set for its return
Blinded eye absently watching
Failing to show concern
Released from the world
Carrying more than a shade of doubt
Escaping half whole
But you made it out
Wondering aimlessly
Without a sense of direction
Hunted relentlessly
By the demon of recollection
Desiring love
Unable to recognize it
Rejecting your own reflection
Through shame taught to despise it
Projecting a mirage of stability
Foundation erected on a fault line
Internally enduring eternal despair
But without you look just fine
No one has asked

So you haven't need to lie
Your core is dry
So you do not cry
But never allow a soul who would try
To gaze too deeply into your eyes.

Behind the Glass

Behind the glass there is a treasure
Confined by shame; encased in blame
Behind the glass there is forever
Soundless same; unspeakable pain
Of it that saw too much
And hid behind the glass
Behind the glass there is a name
Of that one whose sin began
The resurrection of the glass
That holds it captive in the past
Behind the glass a vow to never
Feel so weak, so soul retreats
Behind the glass, concealment cleaver
They can not take, or it will break
So it must reinforce the strength
That keeps it trapped behind the glass
Behind the glass it goes insane
Because the lie it does maintain
Fester, grows and multiplies so fast
...it suffocates behind the glass.

Daddy's Girl

Daddy never told me
Who I was?
What I was?
Why I was?
Daddy never told me
Do you care for me?
Like I don't care for me
What did Daddy never tell you?
Daddy never told me nothing
He never owned me
Never treasured me
Oh yeah
You pleasured me that night
But Daddy never told me
There was more …
More due me
That I was not to be
Used and abused
So sweet inside I am
But afraid and unsure
Because, Daddy never told me
I was more

She Only

She wanted only to escape
But from herself she could not flee
She needed only to be loved
But that was not to be
She sought only strong embracing arms
To protect her
But there was no man who could
They only did degrade or neglect her
But to cherish her none would
She looked for knowledge
In the unknowing
Searched for wisdom in a fool
In her thirst for kindness and understanding
She suffered heartbreak from the cruel
She tried to light the eyes of the soulless
Bring joy to those who cared less
She was a lamp covered in darkness
But to shine, she did her best.

The Rain Must Always Come

I was comforted gently
Into a calming sleep
The false sense of security
Gave no clue to the sorrow I would reap

The life preserver that I once wore
I sadly know exist no more
I surrendered my love, but you did not the same
Handled my absently then put me to shame

In my world you were as perfect as the sun
But an acquaintance with reality has shown me
That the rain must always come

Through the most turbulent storm
I remained asleep
Then I awoke
Drowning in a flood so deep.

And Still I Can't Complain

I am wondering…
Through a forest dark
Crossing a vast plain
Climbing a mountain high
Then caught by a storm in the rain
And still I can't complain

I am arriving…
In a valley deep
Stripped of my name
But my soul I'll keep
Much to reap from that sowed in vain
Labored long and hard with no gain
And still I can't complain

I am reaching…
For that most distant star
Me, royalty made servant
Strength of will measured in scars
Failed protector of family
Brought to my knees by shame
History, Identity, Legacy
ERASED
And still I can't complain!

Heaven Cried

Heaven cried for us all night
The rain fell constant
No birds were in flight
The trees were entranced
In a sorrowful dance
Their leaves lamented in a steady sway
The moon vanished into seclusion
The sun would not face the day
The brightest among the stars
Failed to appear
A fist of thunder
Produced such a deafening noise
Even the Angels could not hear
Lightening illuminated the sky
In search of a reason
A storm shook the whole earth...
But it was not the rainy season.

My Memory

If I could just touch once more
The brow of my much adored
Memory
But you my memory
I cannot with a worldly grasp embrace
I have in my mind's eye
Every intricate detail of your face
Yet, resting in my arms
Is but a pillow in your place
I wish that I could take hold of you
Sweet memory
I long for you to speak to me
With more clarity
Than your now distant echo
Memory
If you would materialize
For just an instant
I would take hold of you
And remain with you
And follow you
Wherever fleeting memories do go
I would that I could kiss once more
The lost lips of my memory
And smell that faint but familiar scent
You were here one day so vividly
Then in an instant
Away my beloved memory went
At times you draw me forcefully

Into a time that is no more
Then sometimes you stay away for so long
I think, I do not know you anymore
Memory
Why can you not
Ever again be flesh near my flesh?
At best all I have left
Is recollection
And a soul connection
But the manifestation is gone
And I am alone
In my dreams you seem
To be once more whole
And I reach for you
Though I cannot feel you
Still, I plot from within a dream
On how to from a dream steal you
With the break of day
Life takes me away
From the lie
That could not have been more true
The tears of my soul remind me
My memory, of how I do love you
Through remnants of you
I try and fuel you
By adding dissolving detail to you
But these remnants
Do at times my heart tear
Reminding me that indeed you were
But will never again be here
Memory

Can you wrap the full of your arms around me?
And not vanish with a dream
After with me the night spending
Then memory would you leave me please?
So I can turn my weeping eye towards mending.

His Rose

She was a budding rose
Nestled in among the thorns
Her petals held a radiant hue
Having weathered the storms
Still her stem was not worn
Not ever a rose held beauty so true
If you owned the garden what would you do?
She was but a budding flower
Absorbing by day the rays of light
Promising to bloom within the hour
Then vanishing on one August night
The sweltering heat was quickly rising
And the fog was growing thick
She would have grown until she wilted
But she was His rose to pick.

In memory of Aaliyah

54

Leave Me to Dream

Do not wake me from my dream
Reality only seems greater
Let me sleep away time if I will
Try and join me later
But do not wake me from my dream
A palace awaits me in the sunrise
Shimmering gold dust stirs in the breeze
Right before my slumbering eyes
Honey drips like nectar from the leaves of the trees
Please, do not wake me from my dream
Leave me to paradise
Go on with life
In my absence do not fear
I have found my place
I'm happy here
Do not wake me from my dream
The mountains sing a song of praise
At night the stars fall and greet me with a kiss
My days are bliss
I do miss a few of you
But if you truly do love me
Then do not wake me
Allow me peace
Release me
The Dream Catcher is calling me by name
Rose petals are strewn about for my reception
I am to be free in this domain
He has awaited my return since conception

Leave me to dream
Go on with recollection
Do not cry at my rest
I feel no pain
My thirst is quenched
By the morning after rain
Do not stir me from my dream
I have no want to wake again.

Our Last Embrace

Remembering our last embrace
I cannot conjure
The full of your face
On that moment I was lost
In our last embrace
A flood overtook me
Its tide heavy and clear
Never again would we two
Be so near

Our last embrace
Came as a thought second
Parting as usual
But the spirit beckoned more
Our eyes caught
And as magnets we sought
And not fought
The force of attraction
Being unwise
To the cause of our reaction
Our last embrace
Should have went on and on
But hurried by life
You too soon were gone
And I went on…

Unaware of the waste
In our haste

On all, had I known
I would have held on
When last we embraced.

Until We Meet Again

Staring into clouds
Even on the clearest night
I see you
And cannot reach you
Therefore, I write

I feel you watching over me
As our eyes lock by a distant chance
The wink of a star is our communion
Serving greatly to enhance
The bond known only to us

Oceans of life removed
Separate our wanting embrace
The sorrowful longing for reunion
Is painfully evident in the space
Of our denied manifestation of love

Memories, alive and well
Though within my heart dwell
Do no longer sustain
But are all of we that does remain
…until we meet again

Displacement

Why do I continue to look for you?
Deep with in another's eyes
Another's lies
Another's smile
Knowing all the while
That of you no replica could be made
You were sprung from material more rare
Than ancient jade
If ever a shout of resemblance is heard
It is always a far cry
Still to draw semblance to you; I try
Why do I compare any to you?
And dare not look through the façade
Of that which does masquerade as you
When no one could to the soles of your feet
Measure up
Why do not I just give up?
An accept that there will never be another you
And suffer the recognition
That there is not supposed to be another you
When ever I think a copy to be most true
The illusion is vanquished by this faintest memory of you.

Here That Day

I met an angel here that day
He was truly heaven sent
Our paths crossed for a brief instant
At best it was for only a moment

On Earth the angel could not stay
But there were a few things
He needed to say
So he stopped by here that day

My angel was a prophet
The knowing weighted his mind
He had an urgent message to relay
But he owned a lack of time

My angel was sent with great reason
But reason not realized
Until the wrath of hate and violence
Snuffed out the light
In my angel's eyes

And my heart to this day cries
You see, I loved the angel
I met here that day

His soul was pure
His being conflicted
To know him was to know love

And the pain his end brought with it
His voice was resounding music
He spoke the word of a poet
I met an angel here that day
But, then, I did not know it.

For my Memory

The Tragedy

Two lovers overcome by the purest emotion
Souls wanting so to join
But fear intercedes against devotion
And the one would not come
And one's heart was stung
Because it needed that one someone
But the one would not come
So alone the pair did part
The one closed off
The other left of heart
Toiling of why the one's love failed to start
Then that one closed, cracked and began to feel
Fear lost the one its love
And with absence the one's heart did reel
In love, overwhelmed the one did kneel
Since the one had began to feel
But that one left of heart did not heal
And that once stung became numb
Then that one could not love the one
When finally the one had come
And a tragedy to soul was done.

Why So Soon? (A Dialogue with David)

As the rain falls upon me
Yes, I can feel your tears
Why did you leave so soon?
You were just a child in years
I understand that you had to go
But there is one thing
That I must know
Why so soon?

I took it for granted
That you would forever be with me
Why did you have to leave?
Yes, I realize the Lord has set you free
But why so soon?

The pain
It must have been unbearable
But I still need you here
I know that does sound terrible
Couldn't you have stayed
A little longer
Just a while
Until my heart was stronger
But why did you leave so soon?

If only I had time to prepare
I know, going, it wasn't by choice
But it hurts when I call for you

And you are not there
What I wouldn't give to hear your voice
I just wanted you to know
I miss you
It is not fair that we had to let go
And I still don't know
Why you left so soon?
You had to
That I know
But why so soon?

For David

The Betrayal of the Sun

Leaves continue their autumn descent
The air left of moisture, is dry and chilled
And I have but to think on a time before recent
When all the days were with light filled

The fire dances within the hearth
Still, I feel not touched by its resonant warmth
Doting on much, that is the least not worth
By cooling affection discarded and much accursed

Though the dying landscape is rich in color
I would that could only the rose have stayed
The sun for its season a most awesome lover
Through the fall a romance with summer's betrayed.

For my Memory

Midnight

Lying under midnight skies
Gazing into midnight eyes
Feigning belief in midnight lies
Then those many mournful midnight cries

Caressing the ripple of midnight's skin
Absorbing the fullness of midnight's sin
Lost in the fragrance of midnight then
Craving the midnight again and again

Weakness is strongest at midnight's wake
Worshipping midnight for midnight's sake
Sacrificing to midnight all it would take
Then abandoned by midnight just as the day breaks.

Choking On The Past

I feel like I'm choking
On a huge chunk of past
Scarring my pallet
Like a mixture of crushed glass
And I can not breathe
The mess of yesteryear just won't leave
My fears of that gone
Again becoming
Mind numbing thoughts
Ifing and a but- but- but
Stopping me from becoming
All that I ought to be
My bastard past won't free me
Envious of those moving
Chasing the life
That I believed I was pursuing
When I'm just turning with a motion
Similar to screwing
But not in
Counter to the clock
Undoing
Receiving a shock
From that which was never even bolted
As the voltage passes through me
I am jolted
And revolted
Visions streaming through my head so fast
I'll die if I don't throw up this huge chunk of past.

Mister Non Committed

Mister non committed
On the felonious charge
Of carrying a concealed heart
You are hereby acquitted
Count two
Possession of a genuine conscience
Will be thrown out
And not considered by this court
For lack of evidence
Count three
Laundering your ill ways
Organizing your life
High level racketeering
Could not be proven to the court
The witnesses kept disappearing
As for your previous conviction
For a humane desire to do good
It was overturned on appeal
The guidelines set in precedent
Were misunderstood
So mister non committed
I can no longer hold you
The court apologizes for any hassle
Now, if there is nothing further
You are free to go.

The Game

Forfeit the game
Play it out, why?
It forever ends the same
Scoreless with confusion
Shutout in pain
A frustrated soul
Clock strikes double zero
Down without a goal
Blame given; none taken
Losing column expanding
The more confidence
In self is shaken
Then the heartbreaks
Impact more devastating
Than a 5.0 earthquake
But harder to take
Because there is nothing to brace
The game was designed for play by fools
Though many a foul are called
There has not been written rules.

Who Are You?

Who are you?
That I awake to
In the light
I recognize you not
Though in the night
I had surrendered my lot
But to who?
Are you friend or foe?
Joy or woe?
Unsure, yes of that I am certain
Loving who I do not know
Not much could be worse than this
Is that kiss
You place upon my brow
One of life or death
Are you gift or theft?
When you siphon
What you will of me
Would you allot a drop be left?
Drawn into your gaze
I fail to decipher lie from true
My sight is all of haze
And I am wondering…who are you?

I See You Weep

I know u weep 4 me
I watch u when u sleep
Searching fleeting dreams 4 me
Unconscious tears they stream 4 me
U grasp when u awake
The weight that night did take
U wipe one from your eye
Then u tuck away your cry
Once more your feet do touch the floor
Dress and then head out the door
U smile and hope no one can see
How inside U weep 4 me.

Not I

Envious of I...
For a binding ring envelops my finger
And links of precious metal
Form a chain around my neck

Die to be like I...
For I sink by night
Into a bed of the finest feathers
And lay shroud
Under a sheet of silk

Sacrifice you for I...
Am contained
Behind an iron fence
Secluded from all
But whom I choose to entertain

Covet what am I...
Because my flesh is perfected
And I am claimed
By the whole of the earth

Better to speak you not of I
For I am not longer I

Live you not for I
For I have already died
Grieve you not for I

No soul remains inside.

One Soul Who Cried

Happiness was just an illusion
Sheltered; lacking hope
I unpacked in confusion

Settled in; blended
Completely with a lie
Comfort, but no peace
I lived and had long died
Since no one knew
There was but one soul who cried

With no inspiration
I soon ceased to dream
A future; without faith
Casting a shadow, yet unseen

Just a shell
My once vibrant core withered
Success; absent love
I froze, yet not shivered
And to the Heart Who Listens
I prayed to be delivered

Do not I deserve to again be whole
Can not I reclaim the peace that fear stole?
Will not I be loosed from a silent lie?
Or must I remain.
-But one soul who cried

Trapped

Fleeting memories of days past
Cause me to think of that love, last
And why it did not

Seemingly, I am meant
Never to understand now
Until it is then and somehow
Becomes ever so clear

Longing for the better which is quite gone
Reliving dreams that once right went so wrong
And cannot come undone

Lying in my bed of thorns
Stuck, unable to move, I am torn
Wanting desperately to escape and be free
But I can not seem to release you from me.

That's My Song

Tears fall like acid
On my cheeks
Wanting to explain
My pain
But I have no strength to speak
The circular cycle unchanging
In spite of all my life's rearranging
I end up in the same spot
Looking for love in hate
Praying for a spiritual mate
While I allow the antichrist
To take me through hell
Now I dwell
Where I desire not to be
Blinded by a lonely flesh
I try to patch the hole in me
Wondering where I went wrong
Knowing inside all along
But, hey, that's my song
It's the same
Replicated lyrics
A new name
The tempo is slightly faster
My favorite soundtrack for disaster.

Error of My Ways

I am in love
With the error of my ways
The rain in my days
The trip in my step
The problem missed
I am constantly in search
Of the stray path
In which to take
And then I get pissed
When I am led exactly
Where I decided to go
I am addicted to confusion
Crave the lie
Ache for the illusion
When creating my reality
My material is fantasy
A day dream even
It never lasts through the night
I dance to the skipped beat
Connect to the breach
When I find myself on shaky ground
It is for instability that I reach
I delight in adversity
Panic in peace
I anticipate the disruption
Of my serenity
And count the agonizing moments
Until my tranquility should cease

I have an obsession for chaos
A passion for loss
A sweet tooth for bitterness
A warm spot for frost
Indecision is my weakness
Enlightenment strains my eyes
When I rekindle the flame of my sorrow
Do not expect for me to cry.

Can I Blame You?

Can I blame you?
For not giving me
What I never told you I needed

Can I scold you?
For being the same man who
Caused my spirit to scream warnings
That before this moment went unheeded

Can I appeal to you?
To morph into something
Beyond the limits of your composition

Can I beg you?
To understand me now
When you lack the compassion to listen

Can I expect for you?
To become the man of my dreams
When you have none
And it seems
That mine you have desired to snuff

Can I fault you?
For believing that I
Had totally bought your game
When I never called your bluff

Can I accept you?
For the person that you are
Keep running with nothing
Until I have gone too far

Or will I stop?
And remember me
Splash cool water on my face
Clear my eyes that I may see
Strike a match and re-ignite
My dreams with the flame
And sever all ties to the emotionally insane.

Heart of Stone

Heart of stone
Devoid of sensation
Destined to die alone
Wondering and hoping for not
Destroying the sent blessings
Through grace God did allot
Accumulating treasures
To treasure soley for pleasure
Never to appraise its worth
Time spent here on earth, wasted
Never cared much what you did
Or did much that mattered
Purpose to collect souls
Leaving your prize bruised and battered
Pollinating the world with your seed
Never tending the soil
Lending your crop to spoil
While your eyes affix on greed
Discerning only your needs
Yes indeed
Heart of stone
There is a bone to be picked
By The Almighty undaunted
By your tricks
Whose judgment is swift
So quick
Make amends
Bring you destruction to an end.

Insomnia

Contemplation of disasters
That cease to be
Recalling the recognition
Inside of me
Wondering endlessly
Nobody's anybody
Just me
Wanting to lay my head
In comfort
But nothing to support it
But a rock
Falling into dreamlessness
Lulled by no sound
But the tick of the clock
And louder it becomes still...
Peace escaping through the cracks
Tossing, striving for comfort
But I can't seem to get
This monkey off my back
And louder it becomes still...
Turning from head to foot
Then trying it crosswise
The ticking once thought rhythmic
Now a taunting to be despised
And louder it becomes still...
Meditation scenes of daisies and lazy days
Turn chaotic
Mind racing from past

To future
To now
And nothing can stop it
And louder it becomes still...
Wanting to get out and go
But to where I don't know
So I just lay with my head
On the rock
Hating the tick of my clock
Tossing and turning
Yearning for release
Learning first hand
How elusive is peace.

You're Blues

Yeah I know you
Blues
Shape change
Fear
Anger
Absent
Removed
A chameleon
Yet still I see clues
Succubus
Coveting what is us
But can't quite get there
And now worse for the wear
Damned the earth, unfair
One surely cannot
Return back the clock
Had your share of hard knocks
As did I
But I instead hit the lab
And learned how to box
Ahhhh
What you crying about?
Not the way you planned it
So now you want out
And where might you go?
Tired of Sire denying you, no?
Recollect it was you
Who chose him that be low

You've fatally faltered
Bartered away all control
You ask
Yeah I know you
But Blues
Where's your soul?
Blues
Where's your soul?

Crossroads

Standing in the midst
Of roads that cross
Destination clear
At the start of my journey
But now it seems
I am lost

I have tried to recall
The turn I took wrong
But I have been traveling so long
I am weary
Silent I stand
In this uncharted land
I would yell
But then no one would hear me

I look upon the ground
Beneath my feet
Three paths lead to chance unknown
One would cause my steps repeat
If of what lies ahead a glimpse be shown
I would not fear going this road alone

I am not such a fool to blindly roam
But I dare not turn about towards home
Darkness has covered my way from sight
My feet fail to move
They have stayed with fright

I shall lay me down in the mist tonight
Gather my strength and wait for light
When the sun overtakes the moon by day
I will know to where I had set out
I pray.

Mate of Soul

If ever there was a sky too gray
A sorrow so real
Today be that grave day
Oh, understanding escapes me
At the moment present
Is only the recollection of a distant time
So close to now
Yet further than the initiation of an eclipse
Darkness inescapable
Due to the comfort created by the shaded glare
But alas! I long for the light
The tide may change
Seasons as well
But something stagnate lay within me
Move! I command the deaf ache
Of which I have ownership
But lack greatly control
My walk is intact
Steps ordered
Yet called back
By my unrelenting mate of soul
Acceptance eludes my grasp
Ever fleeting
Never to be truly possessed
Like you
Even as I navigate the ocean's wide
Eyes locked solely on my destination
The undercurrent calls to that place within me

Hidden and known only to he
Who was lost during journeys past
My travels oppose gravity
Whose force although balanced
Pulls me off mine
So strong that but traces of the self
I was once move on
And yet truly not.

Stranger Passing Through

I saw you lying
Under a Cypress tree
A dream figment made flesh
And meant for me
Skin of bronze
A chiseled frame
Hat of straw
Love what was your name?
Like sculpted art
Facial features so intricate
Cherokee bone structure
African lips
And those eyes
Yes, those eyes
The moon's ray
Gave off the light
By which you read
A massive root escaped the earth
To supply a pillow for your head
I was terrified to approach you
Struck dumb for words I'd say
I ran down by the river to watch you
Hidden, where until you left I'd stay
Failing to sleep
I prepared myself with what I might say
I left home early
And sought you that next day
I combed the whole town

But you were no where around
Heartbreak with reality soon set in
My love I was not to see again
Maybe it was for the best in the end
But had I known that you
Were just a stranger passing through
I might have summoned the courage
To rest awhile with you.

Dear Heaven

How beautiful are you?
My Heaven
I have no memory of thee
Surrounded by injustice
Death
Despair
My Heaven,
Please come for me
I want to dance with the Angels
Walk your streets paved in gold
Dear Heaven,
I know you're out there
This savage world has turned so cold
Why did I have to depart?
My divine Heaven
Certainly, I was cozy and content
I never chose to leave you
My Heaven
For what reason was I sent?

Hollow

When first I met
Your gaze
My soul took a pause
Dazed was I
But that with all
I sought to hide
Either from fear
Possibly pride
I continued my stride
But my heart stayed frozen
You it had chosen
To follow
So on I went…
Hollow.

Blue Melody

I am listening to a blue melody
Remembering when we were still
Wondering why that we can no longer be
I refuse to heal
The base line calls to mind a time that is now
When my sorrow seems somehow infinite
And I cleave to it
Repeating my blue melody wanting never to end it
With hold of my sorrow I deny that we ended
What have I left of you if my heart is mended?
There, in my blue melody lies a soulful voice
It fills my ears and stings my eyes
Announcing my choice to stay forever brokenhearted
Mourning my love loss before it even started
One blue melody for my dearly departed
I have no want of a brighter reality
Just let me be with my blue melody
Or turn this just me back into we
If you can not then leave me to grieving
Stop trying to deceive me into believing
That my pain will pass
I hope at least this will last… you did not
I don't want to make it past the pain… It's all I've got
I am alone and who's to blame
A faceless thief without a name
Who caused my love to leave in vain?
I rely on my blue melody
When it has ended I can always press play again.

Hold To Love

I have come to share a lesson learned
Through trial and loss its truth affirmed
That if love lights upon your hand
Take hold of it while yet you can
Do not be quick to let love go
Lest momentum have its innate show
For days they move and time be swift
And cares could sift away your gift
You mustn't tempt sweet love to wait
While on trifle things you hesitate
Attend to love to yield it lasting
A moment come, is ever passing

Where is My Light?

How do I say what it is for you I feel?
This ever expanding love in my heart is real
I have been keeping back this flood for so long
But when I looked for some relief you were gone
Hidden love have scorned my heart
I want to reveal my all to you
But where are you that I may start?
My light is hidden in secrecy
I want to fill you to overflowing
Would you release me?
To what else should this love I give
It must find its place that the whole would live
My love will not cease its fervent growing
But it is all in vain without you knowing
Where are you?
That my love cannot reach
No gulf is so wide
Do not be lost in the breach
If you are falling
I am strong
Take my hand and hold on
I am wasting here alone
Where is my light?
That my love be shown.

The Drifter

Like a shepherd-less sheep I roam
A visitor of countless lands
Still, no place to call my own
Blown about like a fallen leaf
On the wind carried and tossed about
Not but the earth to catch me

I am the drifter

Villages encountered along my way
Offer up rest for the night
But do not allow me to stay
View me an outcast
Connections made plenty
But none do last

So on I drift

Caravans pass by but none offer me a lift
Since I travel light my lone stride is swift
Where to that I am headed I do not know
I have seeds aplenty in my garment
But no field in which to sow

I am the drifter

So I drift on like a river drawn log
Waiting for the overcast to dissipate
And to be seen, then retrieved from the fog.

Notice Me

Notice the force behind my smile
Or the space within my eye
Notice the silence in my noise
Or the thirst for truth in my lie
Notice what makes me seek the light
Within which I hide
Notice the depths of brokenness
Seeping through my pride
Notice the anonymity sought
Though many know my name
Notice the expense that I bear
To cover up my pain
Notice the anger spewing from me
That masquerades the fear
Do you even notice my absence at all
Although I stand right here?
What is it that you say that I am?
Do you call me by what you see?
I have buried myself, inside of myself
Screaming don't notice me.

Journey

I laugh
Because the tears won't fall
I stall, trying to avoid the inevitable
But still the end comes
Why me?
I ask and the answer remains
If not you, then who?
Should it be
That I am spared the pain
And struggle that is my life
I wish that it were so
That I did not have
To endure these times
But if I wish to have time
I must suffer it
To taste its sweetness
That may come sparingly
But always comes
After all
When I fall I feel pain
But I do feel
Pain
Is a unique sensation
Afforded only to the living
Whom I want to remain among
So until my time comes
I will continue on
My journey.

Out loud

Nowhere is left to run
Not a crevice remains
In which to hide
Lodged within a corner
I can feel evil at my side

A panic rises inside me
With a breath its hold I do abate
Do I with all rush blindly forward
Or should I wait?

I cannot let this terror consume me
Though an overwhelming urgency looms
Evil has yet to set its claws upon me
But I know salvation must come soon

Clarity does arrest my being
Even as the massive darkness begins to crowd
I silently commence beckoning unto my Father
Then I call His name out loud.

My Truest Weakness

Memories of a painful past
Will not allow me to go forward
Toward your open arms
My path I wish to direct
But fear restrains me
And the knowing
I could easily get absorbed
In the world of your embrace
Become a reflection of your face
Without a defined place
Of my own
I must stay grounded
Can not afford to be swept away
I require you
Just as the blood coursing through my veins
Familiar souls
Duo when entwined
Rhythmic hearts beat the same
Fearing chance
I deny you the knowledge
Of my depth of love
While risking bliss, I can not reveal
To you what I feel
Strong in everything but this
I must escape you
My truest weakness.

Hesitant Love

Initiation of love
Springs forth anticipation
But with age increased
So follows hesitation
Love's ending
Whether amicable or not
Will harvest pain
Maybe causing one numb
To pledge off love again
Love cultivated in pain
May grow bitter
Trashing hope's plot
With accumulated litter
If mishandled too many times
Love may try
To mate with reason
And upon rejection misplace its mind
Love may escape the dam
As flooding tears
When by God it still can cry
Hollow love may thump and ache
Though its tear ducks be dry
Love may make blind
Waking moments
With just one sight
Forgotten love may seize the subconscious
Haunting defenseless dreams at night
Love may set the coldest heart

Ablaze with its fire
The accountable may not be
Denying all caution
In the acceptance of desire
Hesitation will try its hand
But at last it will not last so long
Love will not be stilled
For all the wariness on earth
It has an appetite too strong.

I Will Not Cry

Not a single tear
Escapes my eye
The dream has been shattered
Still, I cannot cry
Through a pen I tremble
Delegating thoughts to symbol
As I write
What is right?
If I travail through the night
Will I prevail in the light?
The sight of glimmering hope
Is afar
But by far
Not too far off
That old adage about the stars
And the moon
If shooting, soon
I will fly
The dream has been shaken
But I will not cry.

Love

Love
And the meditation of
Love
Does invade my mind
Having prayed in time
To have that which I long for
Needing not much material
But starved for more
So sure it is to be had
But the search
Has me nearing mad
I am lost
Could you light the way to where
Is there?
Never mind the cost
Are you that of which I speak?
My soul has been deprived
I am weak, but alive
Weary, yet my thoughts flow clearly
Show me you
Love
Love, do you hear me?
If yea, radiate from your source
Bright on my way
If not today
Then the next day
But do not let pass away
Too many morrows

Without love
Not be left but sorrow
Love, if you speak
Say that you will have me
Love, if you judge
Do deem me worthy
Love, if you see
Keep a watch over me
If I become too meek to seek you
I will be stayed waiting
Love
Come find me.

In My Dreams

I fell in love with you in my dreams
As unbelievable as it may seem
You crept into my unconscious mind
And discovered a place
No other could find
You courted me there
Innumerable times
Until, I fell in love with you
In my dreams

In REM sleep we first met
And there sowed the seed
I sensed your pure essence
And revealed my true needs
We spoke not a word
Yet understood each other clearly
Over and over the dream occurred
Until, I awoke to love you dearly

So right then
When I saw you there
In my waking moments
I could help but to stare
My behavior was strange
But how to explain
That I had loved you so long
And had just learned your name.
-For T

In My Dreams (Part II)

As I made my way towards the door
The strand linking our hearts began to stretch
I wanted to be found in your arms once more
But you closed the door
And I felt the latch catch
On we went our separate ways
Connected by a string that from strain does shake
I feel the vibration as I walk through my day
Trying not to imagine the pain of the break
So I steady myself through the force of the shake
Hoping and praying that though there be space
Our bond has strength enough
To enforce the cord
And our separate paths will again interlace
That I would be found face to face
With the one I adore
Though the moments are passing
Let our love be called lasting
And in your absence this fasting
Bring me closer to you
In all that I do I carry with me you
Joyful and blue do my thoughts range
While missing you
And far from reality to most it would seem
I visit you often where we met
In my dreams.

-For T

The Matchmaker

The Matchmaker formed my lips for you
Curved my hips and enticed you
Into the newness of covenant love
He ordered my steps and set my feet upon a path
Shared by you
We two at opposite ends but at last when we crossed
No longer were we lost
But found ready to cover anointed ground
I could not have chosen a better whole than you
Clearly I see
Now that I have recovered the keys to my soul
That when true love comes
The tongue of the Maker will let it be known
I by the Matchmaker was shown
While I was yet deceived to believe
That I would forever be alone
That one would arrive as a gift from the sky
And our spirits would lift on high
And in the Maker's hand we would ride
I was slow to realize
The vision becoming realized
But when I recovered my sight
I saw the Maker in your eyes
And I remembered you
From before the first wave
Washed upon the ocean's shore
From before the moon did glow
Or a blade of grass did grow

I remembered you
From before the sun did rise
And streak the sky with a heavenly hue
I remembered you
From before the first rains did fall
Or ever there was a morning's dew
I remembered you
I smell you in the breath of life
I was called at birth to be your wife
And bring to life a holy nation
Planting seeds enough to grow
And multiply through generations.

As I Wait

When will you come?
The pain is thrashing at my heart
But I will hold my place I can't depart
I want at times to turn and deny you
Sometimes I want to run and find you
But I hold my place I have to try you
…so I wait

What in the world could be keeping you?
I hope you're still walking I'm waiting to meet you
I have to show you how much I do love you
Why have you not come?
I cannot even speak the pain
My eyes release its sorrow's rain
I pray that I will see you again
…as I wait

My soul begins its shuddering grief
I hold to the hope of some relief
I find inside of me some peace
…as I wait

I keep my eye on the larger plan
Your destiny is close at hand
Thinking what if you turned and ran
…as I wait

Hoping you keep on coming on
With out knowing the way of a road so long
Comforting you with the breath of a song
…as I wait

I spy you as you round the bend
Thankful for your journey's end
Another one's to soon begin
But now we're walking hand in hand.

Classical Love

I grasp you in the abstraction of Picasso
See you in the light
Strewn across the subject of a Rembrandt painting
I hear you in the frenzied notes of Beethoven
Drawing images of passion
That now nears me to fainting
I am swept away by your fluidity in Bach
I remember you in a Shakespearean sonnet
Though never before were you remembered not
You sing to me through Solomon's song
Pierce my soul from within a soprano's opera call
You sway me in the breeze of fall
That did shake the leaves of century old trees
Before they were yea tall
I smell you in the scent of a budding rose
Feel your coolness in a rolling stream
I will call you my classical love I suppose
The discovery of you is like waking into a dream.

My Perfect Love

I have longed for a love
That forms poetry with his lips
One that sparks a raging desire in my flesh
With the lightest stroke of his fingertips

I have ached for a love
With the magnetism
To stall time
As I gaze into his eyes
And he into mine
Our souls connect
And we reflect
On nothing but one another

I have prayed for a love
With a spiritual depth
To surpass the measure
Of the Earth's surface to its core
Discovering hidden gifts in me
That I have yet to explore

I have beckoned unto a love
With the devotion of Abraham
A sower equal to Jacob
Purpose likened to that of Moses
As courageous as David

Oh to know love
That can weather torrential rains
Adapt to the changing winds met at sea
A love that can discern my true spiritual self
A perfect love formed just for me.

Ever Lasting?

Ever lasting?
Truth be told
I thought such a word rather bold
A description seductively alluring
Strongly assuring infinity
Would such a gift be granted me
In regards to love
By what instrument would I measure
A love everlasting treasure?
Must I expire before love would cease?
If apart from love may I know no peace?
Must the presence of love be most prominent?
What if love is constant, but distant?
I could go on and on in this very fashion
And still never fathom the full meaning
Ever lasting?

My Familiar

Absence makes fondness in the heart grow
Space separates but longing does bridge the breach
Belonging nowhere save where with all I know
Waiting with patience till said destination you reach

Falling quickly from your gaze of start
Then the stroke of truth in your touch
By passed formality and captured my heart
I slipped into your fold my whole mesmerized
I recognized you, my familiar, by the light in your eyes

You rescued, for me, my long abandoned want
And resurrected much latent desire
That flourished into an aching need
Far surpassing the force of dire

I am anticipating the fulfillment
Of that which our spirits did ordain
I count the passing moments
Until our paths are blessed to cross again.

I Got Up

You stomped
And ground me into the ground
Until I was but dust
But I gathered myself up
That of me that should have went
Was spread about by the wind
But the I did not end
And I got up
You burned me to cinder and ashes
But when the smoke began to thin
I swept the I up
And did not end
But got up
You stranded me in a barren desert
And I went so without
Until my thirst was forgotten
But the I from which I was begotten
Sprung forth a well for I his kin
And reminded me to thirst again
And I did not end
But got up
You wrapped me in plastic
While I still considered you a friend
Dumped me a heap into a trash bin
Labeled me worthless then
Closed tight the lid
And thought there I would end
But think again

Treaded I above disgust
The lid you closed tightly, but not enough
The removal of which was trying and rough
Once free I was soiled
But pleased
I got up.

Authentic Spring

How beautiful are you
That I recount as my truest love?
Now that I do you remember
Before it was my spring that was laced with frost
What since it did make to feel this chill
Rightfully in December.
With the seasons so with proper climate aligned
I could endure the frost that iced at its appointed time
And when at once the authentic spring did come
It brought with it a warmth that thawed
That which the glazing frost did numb
The arctic December wind had left me frozen and dry
The ice sickles encasing my soul
When the season changed began to drip
And the coveted tears suspended in my eye
Slid a path down my cheek and salted my lip
My love did transform that which was bitter
To the sweet
That I would be made again whole
In an authentic spring
Then bask in the summer's heat.

Please Wait Until I Speak

I can't knock you nappy heads
Whether you rock the twist
The shoulder length dreads
Or the crop-top fro
I'm digging the natural style
From atop your crown
For sho
But why you got to put me down?
Cause I got weave to the floor
You presume to know more
Your hair do
Make you stronger?
Blacker?
More true?
No!
I think you need to reevaluate
The way you calculate
Consciousness
Peep this!
Permed hair
Does not a spirit in despair
Make
It's just hair!
Nappy roots is no substitute
For God given
Knowledge or wisdom
Allah
Jehovah

I am
Whatever you call Him
Will be checking solely
For the style of soul
Of those seeking entrance
Into His kingdom
Appearance is a shallow means
Of judging what's deep
Before you assume to know
The level of my intellect
Please wait until I speak!

Stop Dreaming?

I won't stop my dreaming
Want to crush me
Make me Conform
Silence me for being
Not even leaving me space to grow
I will not be contained
Your ghetto
Your ghetto
Keeps telling me no
But I have yet to ask permission
Listen
I won't stop my dreaming
Say what you will
Who are you to believe in?
Bitter tongue slicing air
While I'm striving and achieving
Your reasons
I care not to consider
Churning irrelevance will produce not
But litter
Wither
Where you are if you must
But if in nothing before
In these words do trust
I won't stop my dreaming
You can not restrain me
I will be what I'm seeing.

Ask Why?

Why ask why?
All reason is unreasonable
Yet the irrational shall self rationalize
And accept the same lies
Lacking greatly in creativity
But the aim is the same
To maintain mental captivity

Once more
The pot ain't even black no more
But that stainless, nonstick type of steal
The ever black kettle is pissed
Blowing off steam
Challenging the pot to keep it real

They don't even skip the cracks
When they walk
Forget about the truth
When they talk

Hey, but their English is good
Words easily understood
Educated even
Though when used for deceiving
They still amount to lies

The fancy talk
Serves to sugar coat it

But it is the same ol' bull
Shhhhh!
It has always been

Why ask why?
Search not for sound reason
However, console yourself with this
The wicked shall not reign, but for a season.

To No Avail

Laugh and plot
My way to fail
Curse my lot
To no avail
Sink my ship
On wings I will sail
Murder me with lip
I resurrect and speak my tale
Whatever you think I shall not
Just watch me
I shall.

The Revolution

A song begun anew
Like a morning's dew
The once whispering
Are shouting now
Ancient warriors gaining life
Reborn somehow
The mountains echo with veneration
Evil quakes with trepidation
The revolution…
And everything's stirring
Not a soul is still
The trumpet has sound
From just beyond the hill
The revolution has…
A rumble looming in the distance
Not felt at once
But once felt never to be forgotten
The ocean's shore
Seems calm and serene
But a tide is steadily rising
Call in the rafters or be damned
The revolution has begun.

To The Finish

I am simply coasting
Hoping not to smack the wall
I jump the speed bumps
Even though I fear the fall
I am simply coasting
Giving this ride my all
Aware of where are set the breaks
But them, determined to not apply
Anxiety does my stirring wheel shake
Moving so fast that if I crash I'll die
And still I want to fly
Tired of the slow roll
For once I'm letting go control
Those on the sidelines to afraid to scream
But I am coasting with a dream
Some say this ride is akin to suicide
But I call it life
And I have to try it and glide
Suicide would be to stop and end this
But I'm a hang on tight even if I slide
To the finish.

The Overflow

I prayed one day for falling tears
Because my eyes had gone out dry
Years of weariness and fears
Had worn me till I thought I'd die
Forgive me if you think I pry
Was there ever a time you could not cry?
I knew that if the flood in my soul would just release
I could let go of my turmoil
Take inside of me some peace
What a thief to steal my tears
Leaving me barren for seven years
I prayed to be like those bent in sorrow and in pain
Spent in travailing
Unloading with wailing great burden
Then I could stand erect again
But though my heart was lame
And I was turned out cold in shame
I could not for all I tried
Bring forth a tear from my own eye
I never ceased to wonder why
I had gone so long and could not cry
The pressure at times would so build
Like the raging waters of a dam that won't break
I'd think be still or I'd be killed
The shutters of mourning would my soul shake
When would my pain quota be so filled
To surpass containment that my tears be spilled
Then I prayed one day for falling tears

With a touch I felt a rising slow
How surprising you must know
When my once barren eyes let the first drop go
It into healing ground did sow
And it was followed by the overflow
...it was followed by the overflow.

The Buried Treasure

There lay deep beneath a buried treasure
Chained covered with dirt on a rock in the sea
Not much anything could survive there for long
But it was lodged for what seemed like eternity
Then a storm passed over
And the fierce wind were wrought
A current went out and troubled the water
And loosed the treasure that was in the sea forgot
The sunken treasure began to rise
The waters were dark for miles ahead
It continued to be drawn up on high
Until it was lighted by the sun
That pierced the water from the sky
The buried treasure broke through the surface
And could not be called as buried anymore
The current continued to drive the treasure forward
Until it rested against the sands of the shore
There lay the treasure that was lost in the sea
In plain view to be found on the shore... by me
When I opened the chest what inside I did see
The current had retrieved what I had lost in the sea
For what seemed like more than eternity.

You Turned

You turned to me and heard my cry
From deep within the void of sorrow
Just at the point I thought I'd die
You turned and promised me tomorrow
You gave great vision to my eye
And birthed inside of me a song
You leaned in close and whispered gently
What you had been saying all along
You turned and placed your hand upon me
And revealed those secret things with love
That long denied I then could see
When to me you inclined from above
You covered me and made me new
And healed all brokenness inside
Put in me you and then I grew
You turned and heard me when I cried.

Song of Praise

I sing unto you a song of praise
Oh you that held me through the night
With morning wings you bless my days
And set me out about my plight

You guide my path and keep my course
And provision along the road you lay
I'll praise you while I have a voice
And seek your face throughout my way

I sing unto you a song of praise
Oh you that held me through the night
With morning wings you bless my days
And set me out about my plight

You clasped your hands around my heart
So it would not grow cold while this journey enduring
When fear tried to quench my very start
Just a glimpse of your promise proved boldly alluring

So I sing unto you my song of praise
Oh you the one who held me tight
And keeps my sight from the smothering haze
Joy prevaileth through the night.

Since I Let Go

I am waiting on You
Finished debating myself
And concentrating on circumstance
To the expense of myself
I am waiting for You
To do what You will do
I am through
Laying my hands
When they are best kept at bay
I am trying it Your way
Lead me
Speak to me
And I will heed
True to Your word
Just let it be heard
Once desperate and in need of an answer
Confused I overlooked You – my Answer
I strained to figure
And make a way from the pain
But my efforts were all in vain
And I became blinded to all hope
That is when You reminded me
Above all to hope
In You I could cope
I wish that I had took hold of You so long ago
But it would not have been as sweet as it is
Since I let go.

My Psalm

Lifting up my light in praise
Amazed to have overcome the night
With intact my plight
Ready to face the day
With clearer sight and a more durable will
My calves You have built up from my first steps
When I dropped into the sunken depths
Among the lowest of Earth
I, You never left
Inbred strength in me enough to climb the hill
Readily steady in You my walk still
You hear when fear hath choked my voice
The yoke You broke
Even when the shell was mine of choice
You resolved to salvage me
From all consuming destruction
I unaware, You revealed truth to my spirit
When my mind was reluctant
Once, steeped in darkness, I saw You not
When the world had turned from me
And would have had me rot
You restored me unto Yourself
I You remembered
When everyone else had I forgot.

The Swan In The Middle Of the Creek

I saw a swan watching God today
It stood quietly in the middle of the creek
And did not once set apart its beak
It made no attempt to speak
But just stood there quietly
In the middle of the creek

The wind blew past it
A chilled one from the west
The swan stretched out its neck
To steady itself
All the while admiring
The splendor of God's wealth

It stayed there motionless
And made not a sound
Mesmerized by the paradise
Which it had found
It did not move
For what seemed like forever
Praising God in its stillness
A simple swan, but so clever

The water rushed past it
Both that way and this
The swan was neither bothered
Or worried
While caught up in God's bliss

138

The swan turned its head
In every direction
Absorbing the fullness of God's glory
Then I made a connection
Though two very different creatures
On that most beautiful day
We both stopped to praise God
In exactly the same way

But I on the shore
And the swan in the middle of creek.

Thank You

I know that You are constantly
Righting wrongs for me
Showing me realities
That before I failed to see

You have lifted the veil of my existence
And at once set me free
Reminding me through what I am not
Of what I am called to be

Catering not to my whims
But instead to Your will
Greasing my face to prevent frost bite
When sending me into the chill

Then shining Your light so brightly
The glare is surreal
Directing me home before I have lost
All sensation to feel

Replenishing spent strength
Before my spirit would be killed
Returning seven fold
That which the enemy did steal
Then setting your hands at once upon me
So that my wounded self be healed

I thank You with my soul
For never turning away your face
No matter how low I sank
You met me there with grace

Unconditional love to me at birth
You mercifully gifted
Just thinking on Your awesomeness
My heart and soul are lifted.

The Beach

A current did my boat capsize
Occupants turned out amidst a vengeful sea
Those that could swam vigorously for life
Not a soul resigned to sink, save me

Never a swimmer
I exclaimed that I would die
To say that I had hope
Would be, shamefully, a lie
As the ocean engulfed my mouth, nose, and ears
It increased in its volume with the salt of my tears

Then from ever more rang out a voice
A wash of calmness took its toll
Then out of grace there came a choice
I could opt to stay
But was given way to go

The water did float the branch of a tree
Right there all along I had just to look and see
I outstretched my hands salvation just within reach
I was carried with the waves, on a branch, to the beach.

For Rachel

My Guide and I

Sorrow and loneliness
Became my only friends
I cleaved them snuggly to my bosom
And dwelled where the pain would not end
Wasted from my journey
My eyes fought to not forever close
With I silent of will the guide inside I chose
To direct my way
Onto where lay the light of day
And I stayed and was sustained
Even through the drought
Then a flood released
From He that rested in me
And washed my sorrow out
Through time set aside for my guide spent
Loneliness no longer had a place
And on it went
And with it my pain was sent
My guide did my soul replenish
And through a vision did confirm
I could not have before went finished
Because the place of promise was so near
Then destiny was reached
Now my guide and I reside here.

Just Like Me

I love because I can
I dance because I am
I have died and lived again
And I am not afraid
Walked thru the place of war
Was scarred and bruised
They don't show no more
I live because I do go on
And I am not afraid
What would it profit me to fold in fear?
What else could they do to me here?
That ain't been tried already
Naw, I'll just keep on standing steady
Jump at me and I won't blink
Navigated the gutters
Still I don't stink
That bible verse be more than a quote
Walk the fire, did I, but don't smell like smoke
So they can not intimidate me
Saw more pain than they whole life
By age three
Had pieces stripped from me greater than all they be
And there's still more left of me
Ivy League and class and things
Might make they think they got weight on me
While they was in ballet
I was finding needles where I play
While they was on them swings

I dodged grown men wanting nasty things
While they went for joy rides
One by one, all my homeboys died
But I walked out the ghetto whole
On a promise to blow and I wont let go
Till I get where I'm going
Get in hand what I got coming
Make my mark where all can see
So the other little project "bay bays" can grow up
And be just like me.

Now I'm Gone

Why? I don't even know how to feel
I have no tear drops, Left
This can't be real
Trying to trace the place of my pain
Wondering if I'll smile again
As I strain with shallow breath
With no tear drops, Left
Much too late to be afraid
The course is set, decision made
I can hear me slipping away
And I don't even know how to feel
It's happening so fast…this is real
Nothing can last forever, I know
But I had not planned this day to go
Slow down, please!
My memories are spinning out of control
I don't want to leave…why must I go?
If I could fight, I would
I would grip life tight, stay here, if I could
But I cannot hold on
…I think I'm not alone
No wait!!!...Oh, It's you
…ok
Now I'm gone.

4 Lisa "Left Eye" Lopez

The Promise

Ever Love holds close to thee
And whispers what is soon to be
The bringing forth of promise and
Discovering what lies in your hand

Look into you, see clearer still
The quiet strength, within your will
Will not go waste, move not in haste
Though vision slows, it will fulfill…

Ode to Morning Glory

Oh Morning Glory,
How sweet you are to have come
When darkness seemed
To compass about me
You brought the sun
Morning Glory, your breeze has cooled
The heat from the refining blaze
Your scented air has filled my soul
Dispersed the clouds and cleared the haze
You have bathed me with light
Delivered me from night
Morning Glory,
Just as I am I do embrace you
Your rays have absorbed themselves within me
And granted me the grace to face you
Most beautiful Morning Glory
You are worthy of all praise
My prayer is to forever bask in you
And walk always within your day

Eros & Agape

Eros,
I have been led astray by your scent
Pounding heart, beating wildly
Reverberating with sounds of anticipation
So loudly
That I cannot hear to think
And I fear to think
What I would think, if I could think clearly, Eros

Agape,
You were my friend, my lover, my Adam
My brother
Like unto you is no other
You saw and accepted me
You respected me
You protected me
I found shelter in you, Agape
You allowed me to rest

Eros,
You too many times have authored confusion
I search for a love that is real, Eros
But you mislead me with illusions
You are no more than a smoke screen
That conceals the wisest parts of me
I fell in love with the dream
And awoke in a nightmare
Too doped up to scream

From your effect on my chemistry
But the high is blown now, Eros
And I must leave

Agape,
I return to you
My first love
The one most true
If you will have me now, I am ready
Had I known that Eros was not you
I would have come to you already
Do you forgive, Agape?
Of course you do
If you could not forgive me
Then I would know again, it was not you
But another pretender beneath the mask
Who like Eros only masquerades as you
You have waited for me with patience
And given me space to grow
So kind you kept no account of my wrongs
Even though I had you suffer long
You have never envied me
Nor provoke me, sore
So I return to you, Agape
A true love that is more

I to I (Atonement)

I apologize
For hanging I out to dry
Convincing I of lie after lie
For abusing I in every way imaginable
I apologize for misusing I
Who deserved better
I full of so many hopes and dreams
How could I have allowed I
To suffer alone, while I muffled I's on screams
I made I stay in places where love could not dwell
I on a constant search for heaven
While I lead I into the depths of hell
I apologize
For letting the unworthy inspect I
Knowing they did not respect I
Why did I neglect I?
When it was on I to protect I
I could not see I's own beauty
For that I am sorry
I almost destroyed I
For that I am sorry
I completely ignore I
And for that
I am sorry
I did not even love I
For that I am sorry
I, if you can, please try and forgive I
I have learned many lessons

I am determined to make it up to I
Who I consider I's true blessing
Just writing I a note confessing
How wrong I was to treat I so
I have realized what I have done
And I apologize that I
I did not know
-Love I

The Reconciliation

Star dust shimmering in the iridescence of the moon
Reflecting a promise of the Sun rising soon
The night possesses a beauty its own
Missed through sleep and bliss
But through tribulation shone
Revealing the value of another day to be known
Truth enduring throughout the age
Shining so bright
Now that a moment of darkness has set the stage
Emerging from fright and grief
The remembrance of a once lost Love
Has brought relief
And a peace inside
Unexplainable, yet undeniable
And still viable even in a time of war
And with so many, no more
Millions of tears falling
Summoning the Light
The multitude has one voice calling
It's raining tonight
Soaking the whole Earth's soil
Restless souls tilling through toil
Until the morning wakes
And the fruit of reconciliation breaks the ground
A sound is heard of one returning
Who had before set out alone
The prodigal son has found his way home.

The Eclipse

It happen on a starless night
The sky was black with absence
Out of the void
The nothingness threatened to consume me
Its presence looming from just beyond
Summoning me
I had thinned until only the faintest print remained
A million cast an I upon me
As my fullness withered in shame
I, the lesser light
Under the Eclipse of night
Passed away from all sight
For a moment

The Mask of Passion Kept

Oh what beauty is passion kept?
Hidden behind the mask, I wept
Deep within my soul did sleep
Heady laden with promise that failed to keep

My eyes no longer sought to dream
Silence fought my will to scream
And while numb still did I breathe
Praying for just one to leave

If I could feel my heart would break
How broken am I who do not feel
I had no strength left for that love did take
And take it would love that I be healed.

Remembering You

I find myself remembering you
The one I had hidden in the recesses of the shore
A place that through loss of loves and anguish
I had promised to no more explore

I had put you away with all things desolate
Where dried up dreams and long spent hopes abound
Left in the presence of things meant to forget
A hollowed aching land without sound

I sailed away and glanced not back again
Prayed for my brokenness to soon find its way to mend
Nights spent chasing thoughts of you away
Days passed bidding myself forward, onward
Outdistancing yesterday

But you would not stay left behind
Instead you traveled a current more swift than mine
And now I find myself remembering you
Where currents cross and mighty streams blend
Into a river, strong, whose rolling never ends

Where Have All the Listeners Gone?

There is a knot in my chest
That I want to express
But all I have is my pen
I cannot fit it in a word or two
I knew that from the very start
Still I tried to write from my heart
Until I ran out of ink
When the pen began to skip and thin
I started to think
What a sad way to express my soul
On a sheet of paper with no one to know
Truly how I feel
Writing on my pain alone
Never coming close to describing it
If the truth be known

Where have all the listeners gone?

That I could purge my pain truly
Not just confine it to a song
Where are those with an ear
That I could to spill to?
This sheet won't love me back
When I write until the inkwell's gone dry
The pen notices no lack
It has no arms to hold me
No gentle look to console me
It just waits here while I ache

There is no kiss goodnight from it
No greeting as I wake

Where have all the listener's gone?

Are there any that would care?
Who could offer back a word of ease?
Not like this paper that just lays here
I do not have a large enough vocabulary
To begin to loose this knot
Still I reach for my pen again and again
And write on, it's all I've got.

Goodbye Sorrow

Goodbye to all my sorrows
Goodbye to all my pain
Despair and disappointment
May we never meet again

Fair well to all my memories
Fair well to unrequited love
I will no more linger here with thee
I must see what lies ahead of me

So long my many yesterdays
Today awaits my firm embrace
The cliché has had its final say
I will not another moment waste

It is time that I must take my leave
I have spent all that I spared to grieve
You are too heavy for flight, I long to soar free
Above the cloudy skies of what almost was
I see what I now can be

I Touched the Sun

It was the sun for which I longed
And true to course I blazed towards it
The heat from which did prove too strong
It burned my fingers to the bit.

I was so utterly enchanted
Gave no heed to cautions warning
Not a thing could keep me from it
...Too powerful was my yearning

Flaming sun, my cause of mourning
Beauty great, but such heat to burn
On I rushed, no thought of turning
Until consumed, too late I've learned

Brightest light, what have you now done?
For why did I deserve your spurn?
Alone you shine too be touched by none?
What fault did I who touched the sun?

Eye Contact

Just when I was looking to despise
Declare war, throw in the towel, swear no more
...He caught my eye
I was free-falling, no voice left for calling
Stressed
By so called balling Niggaz who could not see that I'm blessed.
But, instead figure, that with my figure I must be like all the rest
A little cold? Yes. But I must confess
That his eye arrested the onslaught of frigidity
Hum, this fella, had a Stella effect on me
And like the other McMillans...
Just at the point I thought I'd freeze
Our eyes did meet
---and I began to breathe

The Coming of Beauty's Rain

Passion steeped in Beauty's rain
Flood the winding streets again
From that thought to be most plain
Comes a strength that softly gains
Over, under, beyond the course
Which is the path Light does endorse?
Oh show that common thread be great
For destiny anticipates...

Beginning to Blossom

I am beginning to blossom
There is a light for me
A life for me
I am beginning to see
That God had plans for me
Beyond what I could have ever imagined
An inheritance for me
Beyond what they could snatch from me
He's put something special aside for me
And I do believe...it is awesome
I am growing all the while
Not exactly knowing how He moves
But still dancing to the groove
Of the predetermined beat
That swiftly guides my feet
...I am a child of Destiny
And beware; I am just beginning to bloom
Beware haters give me room
Cause it don't stop
And He won't stop
Blessing me
I did not drown in yesterday
I am here right now
Yes, I must say the road's been trying
If I said it was easy I'd be lying
But He turned my mourning into dancing
My night into day
My stumbling into His perfect way

...And I am just beginning

Escape from Eye

If I see myself through the reflection in your eyes
What becomes of I if you look away?
Do I wait and hope that per chance
You bless me with another glance?
Do I pray for you to stay
And never walk away
Lest I fade?
Will I be lost outside the range of your sight?
Might I dissolve in disillusionment?
And come to the conclusion
That my arch descends to resolution
That I am nothing; no more; ended
When I am no more adored; is my identity none?
I will be lost if I dwell in the eyes of one who is gone.
And yet, what if you do not walk away?
But I am still confined within your eyes
My perception of my own reflection
Will surely change as you do,
With swaying moods, the shifting altitudes of life
New attitudes towards...whatever
As you continue to grow and undergo your evolution
Will that be the dissolution of I?
If I become a simple shape changer
Reflected in your eyes
Would the light that had once brightened my days
When you first looked my way,
Have only led me into a cage?
Will I become like the paint you picked and mixed

But have grown to hate?
Will my dreams disintegrate
Into a cloudy haze
Until my due time becomes too late?
No, I think that I will die
If I dwell within the alluring jail of your eyes.
At this moment I do love, in you, my self's reflection
You hold me there like I'm perfection
Hypnotic; is your eye's affection
I feel the force of your pull ...and I don't mean to be cruel
But my withdraw is for my soul's protection
I would go there, gladly, if it could live there
Sadly, it cannot
I am...unattainable
I can not stay
...So, forgive me as I look away.